Communication
Then and Now

Bobbie Kalman

Crabtree Publishing Company
www.crabtreebooks.com

Created by Bobbie Kalman

For Kristof Halasz,

a great scientist in progress!

Lots of love from your cousins in Canada.

Author and Editor-in-Chief
Bobbie Kalman

Editors
Kathy Middleton
Crystal Sikkens

Photo research
Bobbie Kalman

Design
Bobbie Kalman
Samantha Crabtree
Katherine Berti
Samara Parent (front cover)

Prepress technician
Katherine Berti

Print coordinator
Margaret Amy Salter

Illustrations and reproductions
Barbara Bedell: back cover, pages 7 (bottom),
    22 (top right)
Licensed by The Greenwich Workshop, Inc.
    www.greenwichworkshop.com; detail from
    Where Stories Were Told, ©Morgan Weistling:
    page 5; detail from Indian Stories, ©Morgan
    Weistling: page 13; detail from The Barn Dance,
    ©Morgan Weistling: page 19
Wikimedia Commons: Albert Anker: front cover;
    Bonhams: page 7 (top)

Photographs
iStockphoto: page 18 (bottom right)
Wikimedia Commons: U.S. National Archives and
    Records Administration: page 17 (top)
Other images by Shutterstock, including cover photographs

Library and Archives Canada Cataloguing in Publication

Kalman, Bobbie, author
        Communication then and now / Bobbie Kalman.

(From olden days to modern ways in your community)
Includes index.
Issued in print and electronic formats.
ISBN 978-0-7787-0114-9 (bound).--ISBN 978-0-7787-0142-2 (pbk.).
--ISBN 978-1-4271-9413-8 (pdf).--ISBN 978-1-4271-9407-7 (html)

        1. Communication--Juvenile literature. I. Title.

P91.2.K335 2013   j302.2   C2013-906090-1
                                               C2013-906091-X

Library of Congress Cataloging-in-Publication Data

Kalman, Bobbie.
    Communication then and now / Bobbie Kalman.
        pages cm. -- (From olden days to modern ways in your community)
    Includes index.
    ISBN 978-0-7787-0114-9 (reinforced library binding) -- ISBN 978-0-7787-0142-2 (pbk.)
    -- ISBN 978-1-4271-9413-8 (electronic pdf) -- ISBN 978-1-4271-9407-7 (electronic html)
    1. Communication--History--Juvenile literature. 2. Telecommunication--Juvenile
    literature. I. Title.

P91.2.K35 2014
302.209--dc23
                                               2013034932

Crabtree Publishing Company

www.crabtreebooks.com   1-800-387-7650

Printed in Canada/012014/BF20131120

Published in Canada
Crabtree Publishing
616 Welland Ave.
St. Catharines, Ontario
L2M 5V6

Published in the United States
Crabtree Publishing
PMB 59051
350 Fifth Avenue, 59th Floor
New York, New York 10118

Published in the United Kingdom
Crabtree Publishing
Maritime House
Basin Road North, Hove
BN41 1WR

Published in Australia
Crabtree Publishing
3 Charles Street
Coburg North
VIC 3058

What is in this book?

How we communicate

To **communicate** means to share ideas, information, and feelings with others. We communicate by talking, writing, drawing, and singing. How we dress and act are other ways that we communicate. **Devices** such as telephones and computers help us communicate instantly with others near and far.

This girl uses pictures to show the different ways she sometimes feels.

These children are using a telephone and laptop to communicate.

What do you think?

How do you share your ideas with others? What devices help you communicate?

How did they communicate?

People in the past had no telephones or computers, but they communicated in many of the same ways we communicate today. They talked, told stories, wrote letters, read books, drew pictures, played games, and sang songs about their lives. They often shared the news about their communities when they met and talked at the **general store**. The general store sold many of the things people needed.

At the store, men talked while they played checkers. Women learned about new products. People also sent and received letters at the post office in the store.

Body language

People also use **body language** to communicate how they feel. They smile, frown, wave, shrug, and hug. They use **gestures**, or movements, to show certain feelings. What are people on these pages communicating with their gestures?

Is this girl jumping because she is sad or happy?

This boy's eyes are wide open, and his teeth and fist are clenched. What feelings do his gestures show?

What is this girl trying to say using her face, hands, and shoulders?

What do thumbs up and a smile mean?

Showing feelings

People in the past also used body language to show their feelings. The faces of the boys on the right show that they are not happy. The child in the picture below is playing a game called Charades that uses body language to act out words.

What do you think?

What are the eyes of the boys in the top picture communicating? Why is the third boy hiding his eyes? What does his gesture show? What animal do you think the boy in the bottom picture is pretending to be?

Talk, talk, talk!

Each day, people communicate by talking in person or over the phone. There are many kinds of telephones. Some are connected to buildings by wires and only work in those places. **Mobile phones**, or **cellphones**, work almost everywhere. A **smartphone** is a cellphone and a computer in one device.

*This girl is sending a **text**, or typed message, to a friend on her smartphone.*

How do smartphones help you communicate and find information?

Old telephones

People using the first telephones had to call an **operator** to connect them to the people with whom they wanted to talk. Often, other telephone users could listen to their conversations. In later times, people could dial the numbers themselves.

This operator connected telephone callers by plugging in electrical cords on a **switchboard**. *Today's phones are very different. How have they changed?*

Keeping in touch

Today, very few people send letters by regular mail because it takes much longer to communicate that way! Most people send emails or text messages, which arrive instantly. People also keep in touch on **social media** websites, where they create and share information and ideas.

letter

tablet

laptop

The girl on the left is chatting through the Internet with her grandmother, who lives far away. Special software allows them to see and hear each other while they talk. How do you keep in touch with people who live far away?

Mail long ago

Long ago, people did not have email or the Internet for communicating. They kept in touch by writing letters. Sending a letter across the ocean by ship could take months! On land, letters were taken from one town to another in mail trucks or trains. People received their mail more quickly after airplanes were invented.

Mail or email?

What can you send by regular mail that you cannot send by email?

These people, who lived in a city, are mailing parcels at the post office. Mail was also delivered to people's homes, just as it is today.

*These men are carrying bags of mail off a plane. Mail sent by airplane is called **air mail**. Mail arrived much more quickly by air.*

Stories now and then

People love to tell stories. They tell stories about their families and friends, things they have done, and places they have visited. People also share stories in books they write. Pictures help them tell their stories.

What will you write?

Write some stories about your family or about your pets. How will you share your stories with others?

Stories by the fire

In the old days, families spent their evenings sharing stories by the fire. Through stories, children learned about family members who lived long ago. Telling stories was also a way of communicating the **history** of the communities in which people lived.

*This man is telling his grandchildren the story of how the Native people who once lived near his home gave him the **peace pipe** in his hand.*

peace pipe

Sharing knowledge

This teacher is sharing her skills and knowledge of soccer by coaching the school soccer team.

Our ability to use words allows us to share **knowledge** with others. Knowledge can be facts, ideas, information, or skills. School is a place for communicating knowledge. Teachers share their knowledge and skills with students. Students then share their knowledge with others.

These students are researching information for a report that they will share with their class.

What will you share?

What special knowledge do you have that you would like to share with others? In what ways could you share your knowledge?

Learning long ago

Teachers in the olden days also shared their knowledge and skills with their students. Schools did not have many books, so children learned mainly from their teachers. One way to remember the information a teacher taught was to **recite**, or repeat it out loud.

This teacher uses a globe to teach geography.

These students are reciting a poem about history that their teacher taught them. Singing is another way of reciting words. What, where, and how do you recite?

15

Published words

To **publish** is to share the final copy of a book with others. Books communicate knowledge and entertain us. In schools, books are used to teach information about many subjects.

Many people prefer reading eBooks rather than printed books. Which do you prefer?

Your story

Write a book about your life or about something that happened to you. Writing a book is a great way to communicate who you are and teach others about things they may not have known before. Your book could be a big help to others.

Books and newspapers

In the past, there were fewer books, and not everyone could read. Those who could read often borrowed books from libraries. Most children had only one or two textbooks to use at school because books were expensive to buy.

*This student had only one textbook, called a **primer**.*

People went to libraries to borrow books. Students also went there to study.

Communicating culture

We learn about culture from television shows, movies, and photographs taken of people all over the world.

Culture is the way we live. It is the clothes we wear, the foods we eat, and the languages we speak. We share our culture through stories, sports and games, music, art, and the ways we celebrate. How do you celebrate your culture?

This boy shows his Jamaican culture by the hat and hairstyle he wears and the music he plays.

18

Paintings of life

Before there were movies, television, and photographs, people painted pictures to show how they lived. Food, clothing, music, and dance were subjects shown in works of art because they were important parts of people's lives. Paintings communicated information about people's cultures.

This painting shows a barn dance long ago. What does it communicate about how people dressed, danced, made music, and had fun?

19

Learning the news

Today, when news happens in a community or around the world, people know about it right away. **Journalists** are people who communicate the latest information about fires, accidents, special events, wars, and natural disasters. Some journalists write stories for newspapers, and some report the news on television. Most news also appears on the Internet. Sometimes ordinary people capture special events and share it with television stations or on social media.

This journalist is reporting the news on television.

This tourist is recording an exciting news event that he will share on the Internet with friends at home.

News long ago

Before television and computers, most people got their news from newspapers. It took journalists much longer to learn the latest news and communicate it to others. Newspapers had to be printed first. By the time they reached the reader, the "news" was often not that new.

In cities, boys called "newsies" sold newspapers.

When cameras were invented, many journalists took pictures to record news stories.

What's new?

How have television and the Internet changed the way we receive news today? How long would it take to learn the news without them?

21

Do you gossip?

Gossip is a game that was played in schools long ago. To play this game, children sit beside one another. The first player whispers a sentence to the second, who then whispers it to the next player. The last person to hear the sentence repeats it out loud. Often, the last sentence is very different from the first. This game teaches how easily facts can change when information is passed along.

When someone tells you a story, do you share it in the same way with the next person? Do you ever change a story on purpose? Play Gossip with your classmates and discuss how real gossip can hurt people's lives.

Learn more

Books

Crabtree, Marc. *Meet my neighbor, the News Camera Operator* (Meet my neighbor series). Crabtree Publishing, 2012.

Kalman, Bobbie. *How do animals communicate?* (Big Science Ideas). Crabtree Publishing, 2009.

Kalman, Bobbie. (My World series). Crabtree Publishing, 2010–2011.
Some titles include: Rodent rap, Reptile rap, Body talk, My culture

Kalman, Bobbie. (I can write a book series). Crabtree Publishing, 2012.
Titles include: I can write a book about...Butterflies, Countries, Culture, History, My Life, How to be Healthy and Happy, Landforms, "If I could talk to animals..."

Mullins, Lisa. (Breakthrough Inventions series). Crabtree Publishing, 2007.
Some titles include: Inventing the Printing Press, Inventing the Computer, Inventing the Radio, and Inventing the Television

Websites

Learn about the different forms of communication in 1912 at:
http://alookthrutime.wordpress.com/2012/03/04/communication-in-1912-2/

View a timeline showing the history of the computer at:
www.livescience.com/20718-computer-history.html

Learn more about the history of the telephone at:
www2.actewagl.com.au/Education/Communications/Telephone/TelephoneHistory/default.aspx

Words to know

Note: Some boldfaced words are defined where they appear in the book.

body language Gestures and movements showing someone's feelings

device Something invented or made for a certain purpose

cellphone A cordless, portable telephone

clenched Closed tightly

gesture A movement of the body, usually with the hand, arm, or head, to express an idea or feeling

history A record of past events

operator A person who operates a piece of equipment, machine, or telephone switchboard

peace pipe A long, decorated pipe smoked by Native Americans at special ceremonies as a symbol of peace

social media Applications, such as Facebook and Twitter, or websites that people use to connect and communicate with others

switchboard A device used to connect telephone lines manually by an operator

Index